Darker Truths:
Extra Grim Fairy Tales of Even Grimmer Existence

MATTHEW T. MCKEAGUE

No part of this book may be reproduced, transmitted, or stored in any form or by any means except for your own personal use, without the express, written permission of the author. No part of the author should reproduce either, according to the general population.

This is a work of fiction. Any resemblance to actual persons, living or dead, or actual events is purely coincidental. Promise.

Illustrations by Van Gia Hao.

Copyright © 2019 Matthew T. McKeague (First printing in 2016)

All rights reserved. Matthew T. McKeague.

ISBN-13: 978-0-9997901-1-3

DEDICATION

This book is dedicated to all of the trees that had to die in order to make this book...
as well as any lumberjacks crushed in the process.

CONTENTS

1 **Dave Vs. Existence**   Pg 5

2 **Advice From Gramps**   Pg 23

3 **Clean Up Aisle Jen**   Pg 35

4 **Solitary Refinement**   Pg 53

5 **The Greasy Spoon Conspiracy**   Pg 65

Tale 1:

Dave vs. Existence

DAVE VS. EXISTENCE

Dave rubbed his eye gunk, feeling rested quite rarely,
While dazed in a haze, sprayed deodorant... barely.
"Why try hiding a stench that is sure to return?
It's just soothing the truth that my pits always churn."

Impressions aside, no, Dave wasn't a bummer;
His thoughts locked inside like albinos in summer:
"Should I be or not be? Am I really an I?
What is going on here? Will we ever know why?"

He slogged every dawn to his cheap kitchen table,
Which, much like Dave's life, was profoundly unstable.
He'd sneak past his wife and his kids soundly sleeping,
So they'd catch some Z's while he's secretly weeping.

He'd chug coffee mugs and he'd contemplate gloom.
"We're all dying! We're damned downward spirals of doom.
How can folks ever frolic or gloat that they're great?
Don't these doddering dopes realize their cruel fate?"

"Most will get cancer. Some will croak alone shrieking.
The Death Lottery's rigged, statistically speaking.
All the Mayans conked out. And Rome's empire fell through,
And that slow dodo bird, well, it kinda failed too."

When Dave's children woke up, he put on his own show,
Filled with donuts and dread, but they both didn't know.
"I packed all your lunches!" Dave sang kindly, thinking:
"Existence is futile. You kids should start drinking."

His wife bounced from the shower with power and grace,
"She deserves more than my bored and worn, portly face!"
He'd query her feelings and compliment clothing,
While Dave always stayed in a state of self-loathing:

"I am shabby and flabby and falling apart.
From my gut to my butt to my clearly clogged heart.
My memory's fading. I notice more napping.
When I try jumping jacks, my back fat starts clapping!"

Yes, his wife was a catch. She was sexy and kind,
But their hexed daily grind couldn't exit Dave's mind.
She's the love of his life, right beside him engrossed.
Yet, preparing for work barely spared time for toast.

"If we had more cash, there'd be fewer frustrations.
No blissless vocations in distant locations.
All that time stalled in traffic and shifts with few thrills,
Makes us roommates with tax breaks enslaved to pay bills."

This tsunami of thoughts washed on Dave's distraught beach,
So he shared his last "Bye" and he spared her the speech.
"Life's no piece of cake or I must suck at baking,
It's more like a seizure—a jerk that keeps aching."

On Dave's drawn-out far drive in his car catacomb,
He slipped past his last exit and skipped phoning home.
He floored it to stores for some snacks—tax included,
Then zoomed to a bridge that was high. And secluded.

As he gazed at the girders by workers long passed:
"In the grand scheme of things, these will rust and won't last.
When all suns explode, we are done—they will spoil it,
A universe cursed to get flushed down the toilet."

When the moon greeted Dave with his spoon, incomplete,
Freshly half-emptied ice cream pints piled at his feet.
"Life's a joke with no punch-line. A crock, overflowed.
And it's much like this ice cream—one cold Rocky Road."

"But I can't do this here—it's too near the kids' school.
Each bus ride a reminder of Dad the drowned fool.
I'd jump, but they'd want to know why, cry, and quiver.
Plus, since I'm so plump I would empty the river."

His skewed views confused him. "I'm insane and deranged!
How much brain medication will it take to change?
Every second's a struggle—a conflict, a clash,
Each feigned smile a pained trial and it's all balderdash."

Dave aimlessly cruised, under lame constellations,
"Made up by bored dudes with poor imaginations.
They saw humans and beasts, and yet nobody scoffed?
All I see's one big finger that's flipping me off."

He peered and he pondered our squandered potential:
"We fight when our plights might be inconsequential.
All these fake walls and laws we construct for the chumps?
But lock crap in a box—all you have's one safe dump."

"There are billions of balls out there other than here,
Yet the Earth's worth is awesome? We're in the top tier?
We're an orb swamped with water—most that we can't chug.
Such a time bomb with pom-poms. It's bull—pull the plug."

That's when the truck cracked him. Yes, Dave was distracted.
The seconds extended, but his car compacted.
Then he wagged like a rag doll—anatomy whacked,
In death throes, *The Dave Show* played out fading to black.

Dave reopened his eyes in a warm orange blaze,
"Well at least my mechanic might get a nice raise."
Stopped and pinned in, disgraced, flames atop his attire,
The car charred by a vast fast-food wrapper-fueled fire.

For a moment, Dave knew he could end this right here,
By not moving, his bruises would all disappear.
Yet he yanked off his seatbelt and booked out the door,
"I'll be damned if I die like an overcooked s'more!"

He crawled off that tar graveyard and struck softer ground.
His cell melted, he yelled at the truck now southbound:
"Well, I'm bleeding! It's freezing! I may not survive!
I have never felt worse, but as well, more... alive!"

Now lit only by stars, Dave limped through his apt route:
"All this matter is trapped in this wacky crapshoot,
I should laugh at the cosmic cards that we've been dealt.
It'd be dumb to hang glumly from Orion's belt."

A gas station clerk worked third shift as the town snoozed.
Dave slogged in like a zombie, oozing but amused.
"Did you run outta gas?" The clerk's jaw dropped ajar.
"You could say that," Dave claimed. "No more gas. No more car."

On Dave's quest in that cab at illegal, rad speeds,
He assessed our progress and our species' best deeds:
"In the past I'd be pissed on a trip that'd last hours,
With a pox, snake toxins, and ox methane showers."

Dave burst into his house, his kids first shouting "Dad!"
Then he sprung to his spouse, spouting "Honey, I'm sad!
It's not you or the tots—it's a juggernaut force.
And I won't blow my top if we've got to divorce."

"Why did you mask the sadness?" The wife asked, concerned,
"Is that blood mixed with mud? Were your pants, by chance, burned?"
Then Dave sobbed: "I'd be soothed with first aid and new clothes,
Still my grief won't be brief till my flow of woe goes."

"I've kept down my frowns and dejected descriptions.
Inflicted, predicting strict lists of prescriptions.
Yes, I've dwelled far too long in the dark like a troll,
But I see slits of light through this black crusty hole."

Then Dave's plight hit his wife like that truck through the den,
"You're my friend to the end. Please don't pretend again."
They all latched onto Dave like a snugly bear trap,
So ensnared, Dave's despair took a love-induced nap.

Awoke by fine smells and timed bells for swine hissing,
The kids reckoned "Breakfast!" Though B.O. was missing.
Dave then plated wheat pancakes. "You sense my new take?
The chef wore deodorant for everyone's sake."

Dave grouped fruit with coffee and not mounds of donuts,
He quenched his dissent without 10 pounds of cold cuts.
"It's sad life depletes, but eat trash—it goes faster.
Overwrought? Food for thought: Digest less disaster."

Although all the top nurses and all the docs' pills,
Couldn't reverse his curses and fill him with thrills.
Dave still braved through the gray where the bulk of us sit—
Finding nuggets of joy in the everyday shit.

Tale 2:

Advice From Gramps

ADVICE FROM GRAMPS

Gramps wrote in his notebook on his soft hospice cot,
Flanked by his frank family who snored in their spot.
Since old Gramps was a champ at surviving he'd try,
To assist his grandkids with tips how to not die:

"If I've cracked one bad fact on this whimsical sphere,
There are lots of weird ways that we may disappear.
So please heed this advice from my heart without strife,
And Death won't show up early to bogart your life."

"When you're bolder and colder you might try to ski,
But it'd be a disgrace if your face hugs a tree.
Want to stop getting shot with rounds pounding your chest?
Then make sure not to hurt someone's pa in the West."

"If you slay in rage, you could be executed,
So take some chill pills and your fury's diluted.
Your flawed body pod's in a fight against stasis,
So you'd best get tested on a yearly basis."

Advancing in age made Gramps bored of the drivel,
So ancient he's trained in war—foreign and Civil.
He mastered the hazards—some dumb, some insulting,
So Gramps took no chance and continued consulting:

"You will drown when your lungs fill with liquid, not air,
So press on to the desert since moisture's rare there.
Of course you'll get hoarse in those quirky, dry cultures,
So hydrate or your fate is jerky for vultures."

"There's a slew of rude mammals who'd mince your found pounds,
So don't crawl over zoo walls when no one's around.
And if humans consume you, you're burped—they use knives!
So beware those rare tribes and both of my ex-wives."

"On a similar note, you can starve without food,
Though you'll choke on that hoagie if you never chewed.
Snack addict prediction: You'll flop as a whopper;
So fat that your stiff's lifted out via chopper."

That last word stirred Gramps' brain as he yearned for his bikes,
All those slogs through dense fog and ice-covered turnpikes.
Though he smiled about miles of trials more exciting,
He dried his cried tears and supplied some more writing:

"Avoid plague like the plague and stray Petri dishes.
Don't bother the mobsters—you'll sleep with the fishes.
If quartered, you're torn by four swift different horses,
So don't pork that farm girl unless Dad endorses."

"Truth: You get crucified, you'll get cross and can't move;
To refrain, don't make claims that you can't ever prove.
Virgins got tossed in lava to please lots of gods,
Thus, get laid at young ages to ease those hot odds."

"You'll recede if blood leaves your sawed body, flowing;
So don't sleep through school when they briefly teach sewing.
And when crossing the street don't meet cars in your way;
There's no thrill adding 'road kill' to your résumé."

He then mused of loose cruising—no helmets. He sped,
Proudly on his loud hog, now unused in the shed.
Since his window of time and mind were both closing,
He clicked his black pen and went back to composing:

"Trip into wood chippers, your luck could be lousy,
So urge that your surgeon's not prodding when drowsy.
Your head, you lose that, it's called decapitation;
So please keep it stuck in its current location."

"Sunshine summons cells that are hell till you flat line.
And fruit peels near your heels lead to slips and snapped spines.
Take care everywhere of the dangers around you,
Yet, let stress make a mess—you'll be in the ground, too."

"There's impalement, derailment, dumb acts done in love,
Or becoming so drunk you do ALL the above.
But... you know, if you follow my words to a T,
You'll still wind up in bed in a bind much like me."

Gramps closed those envelopes with drying drool dribbles,
And hoped his wise guidance survived via scribbles.
With text to be read and his minutes now numbered,
He went for the shed while his descendants slumbered.

Gramps' bike peeled out and squealed, his blown robe revealed cheeks:
"I'll abort on my terms. They'll report this for weeks!"
And then bound to go down as the town's esteemed stiff,
In his daring farewell, Gramps careened off a cliff.

When the bold news diffused, Gramps' loved ones shared a laugh,
As they scanned Gramps' longhand in his last paragraph:
"But there's one exception that can supersede these;
If past 80, I say, do what you damn-well please!"

Later at Gramps' gravesite, his kinsfolk did chortle,
An epitaph drafted by that badass mortal:
"Inside lies what's left of Gramps' primetime-banned body,
His life flashed like he passed: commando and naughty."

Tale 3:

Clean Up Aisle Jen

CLEAN UP AISLE JEN

Jen tied up her bike tightly slightly before four,
To complete discreet chores at the grocery store.
With her snug rubber gloves on each double-scrubbed fist,
She hoped to grab some grub while her symptoms persist.

"I'll buy verified brands both bland and organic,
Grown local and fresh so I feel less Satanic.
Since the flavor I savor's a microbe that's squashed,
I'll aim for the containers that claim they're pre-washed."

Jen entered tormented. A sign supervised her,
To make the germs squirm with some hand sanitizer.
"While these gels and sheets help me scoop up granola,
There's a 10 percent chance I'll still catch Ebola."

She stole the whole roll of bacteria killers,
Her body's a temple—thug bugs aren't the pillars.
So she wiped off her cart and she started to frown,
Since the store looked much more like a brown shantytown.

"Ew, I see dirty ceilings. The rugs need shampoo,
So I'll use my black light to track mold and mildew.
I've got chow to acquire since my mouth needs feeding,
And desires to retire from viral stampeding."

She insists on no list. "I am saving the trees,"
And she sought only soy, since meat leads to disease.
"I need green leaf-based treats that will make much less waste,
With no gluten, no fat, and, alas, no real taste."

Feeling screwed in this feud, Jen pursued chilled raw food,
Amid grids of crisp vittles, her fear still ensued.
As she routed through rows of the soft rotting fruits:
"Why don't grocery stores also sell Hazmat suits?"

Then Jen turned the corner. Her gut churned, disgusted,
A baker boy worked while (his junk) he adjusted.
He dropped cake! Then Jen lobbed him her memoranda,
Called ***The 5-Second Rule's a Slob's Propaganda.***

Jen fumed past nasty salt-infused soups feeling pooped,
Then fought off thoughts of botulism and recouped.
She squeezed by a mom's spawn sneezing snot from its nose,
And from that, made a pact, to destroy her soiled clothes.

While evading babies, she found coffee supplies.
Hoisting her moist towelettes, she then re-sterilized,
When a wheezing geezer shuffled by, Jen's mind whizzed:
"If he needs CPR, my lips aren't touching his!"

"I'd adore people more if they weren't contagious,
And sharing their air's highly disadvantageous.
They all tackily hack, yak, and linger in aisles,
With their black fingernails and their plaque-attacked smiles."

In dairy, Jen stared at rice milk's expiration,
Dry heaving when breathing near bovine lactation.
She backed up past the jugs and the cartons of crud,
Then bashed into the butcher... all splattered with blood.

"Oh… my… god. I am soggy! Hey, squalor—lay off!
Here comes rabies or maybe passé whooping cough!
Diagnosis: I'm grossest! They got me again!
Hey! Attention, vile patrons! It's cleanup… Aisle Jen!"

On path to the bathroom Jen retched, as expected,
"It transmit! I've been hit! I'm wrecked and infected!"
She quickly kicked down the door like wicked vandals,
Though broken toes suck, they do trump yucky handles.

Then Jen thrashed to the sink and splashed in like a bird,
As soap suds stung her tongue and evoked some curse words.
As she tore off her blouse, doused, bouncing and screaming,
The janitor swore that he must have been dreaming.

"Hey, man with the mop. Can you do me two favors?
Please reach in my purse to converse with life savers;
Call the ER and CDC on my speed dial,
If they say I've been tainted, please buff me like tile."

"I used to be you," spewed the janitor slickly,
Scared parasites prowl everywhere, foul and prickly.
So I picked this profession—I freshen for pay,
With my mop I slay slop, taming life every day."

When Jen glanced at her hands, feeling steamed, seeming drained,
And the Janitor's nametag of Stan—smudged and stained,
She said "You're the man, Stan," as, her mind, these thoughts crossed:
"Stan's too slow. Anaerobes need a quick Holocaust!"

So Jen tossed Stan a tip for his cautious tidbit:
Backup cash she had stashed and dashed lickety-split.
"They so owe you a raise," explained Jen while leaving,
"Please flee before seeing the siege I'm conceiving."

Then Jen toured the store and procured her provisions:
Sponge armor and water guns with fun revisions:
See, now these would eject disinfectant through air.
Thrilled with bleach-filled balloons—this was bio warfare.

Jen's pace to erase pathogen incubators,
Led to shredding the spreading well-fed invaders.
She sprayed like fire brigades. And purged the insurgents,
All colonies falling from girly detergents.

So she lobbed those bleach bombs at each mom and their kids,
Who slid through viscous aisles while they gripped their eyelids.
Mad managers face-planted and missed Jen, rolling,
Dad witnesses deemed the scene worse than bad bowling.

"No relief till deceased. Germs should leave! It's my skin!
Their whole world in my colon will soon be has-been!"
Jen lifted the gun and bit right like a chigger,
With a mouthful of plastic, she pulled the trigger.

As her uvula burned, her taste buds did blister.
Police approached swiftly and slipped—they too missed her.
Jen screamed from the stream of her leaking protection:
"I'm a freak, so to speak, when seeking perfection!"

She exclaimed through the pain, revelation now known:
"I've subdued so much life—and that includes my own.
All the tears. All those years. All the mess being stressed,
More or less helped suppress that I'm sick and obsessed!"

Jen skid on her mission to thwart her aversion,
To squeeze that sick senior with bosom immersion.
"Normally I'd fist bump to miss spores your sores bring,
Yet, I'll let my immune system do its own thing."

Jen raced to the snot baby and got a surprise,
When it puked through the air on her hair and her eyes.
So Jen cackled, yack spackled, to putrid produce,
And ate grapes rife with fungus and traces of deuce.

Then in a hurried blur for the store's checkout lines,
Jen forged to the teen clerk whose hygiene should see fines.
And before he could ask: "Paper, plastic, or tote?"
She stopped him in mid-thought with her tongue down his throat.

Jen came to the next day, chained in jail, pale and ill.
With no vitamins or penicillin to swill.
Yet between fever dreams, her disdain was waning,
"I can't breathe or leave, but hey, I'm not complaining."

Matured by impure tours, Jen spurned her worrying,
As parades of raiders played on her scurrying.
"You can pick your friends, flicks, and defense lawyers' firms,
But you'll lose your mind if you try to choose your germs."

"Like a cannibal loner, you are what you eat,
But life can be quite bare writing off the rare treat.
Some treats are sweet cuisine, while others are mental:
Some minor refiners, others transcendental."

Though locked blocked behind bars, she rebuffed her mind cuffs,
Then she heard "You're free, bird," while she chewed crude foodstuffs.
In mid double-take she did see how she prevailed:
Stan the janitor waving, who paid off her bail.

The allies roamed outside with new tones less caustic.
"Cleanliness is godliness? Nah, we're agnostic."
Yes, they ignored Jen's court date and tried some high-fives,
As they hurdled their burdens with dirt in their lives.

Tale 4:

Solitary Refinement

SOLITARY REFINEMENT

Irvin taped his drapes shut, reinforced them with stone,
Pent up inside fermenting, ignoring his phone.
If you threw him a party, he'd probably moan.
As an amateur hermit, Irv stirred all alone.

At his place every day, Irvin stays and attends.
His escape his quaint home. His five cats now his friends.
"These purring furred felines don't favor the chic trends,
And seldom need help moving couches on weekends."

At dances, Irv ruled with his cool move—spectator.
He'd rehearse to converse with rare dates and waiters.
He'd hike flights of stairs over packed elevators.
And if you said "Let's talk," he'd say "See ya later."

On Mondays Irv murmured his weekly excuses:
"The world out there's scary for wary recluses.
Most humans confuse me. They're rude daring douches,
So I'll hide inside where no one reproduces."

Irv blew Tuesdays perusing the news for breakthroughs:
Why baboons' butts are red. Why his heart was so blue.
With his studies—not buddies—he mused and withdrew.
He grew bright and quite snug as a three-minus-two.

Then Wednesdays—his tense phase—Irv hiked up his hilltop,
If intruders loomed in, his eyeballs always dropped.
And he popped in his earbuds—though duds, worked like props,
That blocked most locals' vocals and made small talk stop.

Thursdays Irv tended cleansing his clothes in the sink,
Sorted toys by their noises and trash by its stink.
On Irv's Friday pet fests were contests to not blink,
And, though his mother paid, he evaded his shrink.

Weekends Irv pretends he's a vet and a groomer.
And shops in his boxers—an online consumer.
Yes, Irv never spread 'more-the-merrier' rumors,
"That phrase needs appraised! What about droughts and tumors?"

His marooned cocoon room became puny with time,
Every week on repeat with each feat less sublime.
"I'm uneven and odd. I will hide past my prime!
I'm no church-bound monk, or worse, some sound-averse mime."

So Irv planned not planning. "And that's a requirement!
Perhaps I can lapse from my silent retirement?
Could I cease or decrease my 'wired in' quagmire stints,
From my home sweet safe zone to strange environments?"

Then on Monday, not Wednesday, Irv altered his core,
He tore outdoors restored, looking up to explore,
Then he tripped on some chick by a thick sycamore,
Where she buckled and tumbled just seconds before.

"I'm so sorry," Irv spoke! "Didn't notice you there."
Yet that did not upset her: "I've heard that. I'm Claire.
I was chasing my cat. She escaped from our lair."
"Hey, no worries," Irv stated. "We'll trace her, I swear."

Those two sleuthed through yarn markets and shops stocked with fish,
Skipping crowds on their trip, as per Claire's fitting wish.
And they mixed stinky fish with chilled milk in a dish,
Which they kicked and slipped into—backsides and pride squished.

All drenched in the moo juice and the fishy debris,
They brushed off with soft yarn, which stuck on instantly.
But then Claire screamed with glee! She could finally see:
Her cat batting at Irv—claws and all, playfully.

So Claire cuddled her cat that purred, rubbing her knee:
"Let's go back and relax. Maybe Irv will agree.
We'll recede and proceed for peace A.S.A.P.
And deter all disturbance with caller ID."

"Our old place. Our home base. Our own tame jamboree!"
Then Irv jerked and perked up. "Holy geez, that's the key!
I won't knock off the awkwardness—she's weird like me!
I declare I'm prepared for a five-minus-three!"

Then they came to Claire's haven. Irv almost fell flat,
When adoring decor—her swell Unwelcome mat:
"In the mood? I'll intrude to view your habitat."
To which Claire shared "No fair! I was gonna say that!"

Sublime on cloud nine as misfit contrarians,
Scorning the norms of the disciplinarians.
They danced and pranced and played veterinarians,
Yelling at levels that'd set off librarians.

The outcasts would last long—sweaty palms, steady heat,
Reading their geek brains out below pillow-fort sheets:
"I like folks in small doses," Irv smirked. "But you're sweet,
You're the offbeat retreat who completes my love seat!"

Flash ahead 60 years. The wed match won't sever,
Stretched out on the couch, unaffected by weather.
Though all right alone, they shined brighter together.
Irv and Claire were a pair. Introverts forever.

Tale 5:

The Greasy Spoon Conspiracy

THE GREASY SPOON CONSPIRACY

"Listen up, sleeping sheep!" Clyde declared live on air,
With his lone microphone, groaning out his nightmare.
Hunkered in his bunker, he deemed all things eerie,
Releasing deep heaps of conspiracy theory:

"Do you find the world loony? Well I'll tell you why.
Most you see is a fake. What *they* say is a lie.
All these sports and reports of celebrity sleaze,
Lets elite keep the masses distracted with ease."

"I must talk about *they* and by *they* I mean *them*—,
Unelected bloodlines architecting mayhem.
They are hitched and on course with the banks, tanks, and tech;
Like a rich person's porch—this is one loaded deck."

Clyde enchanted and ranted a few hours each week,
Then he'd research, immersed in the briefs of the bleak.
Though he lived fraught with fright, Clyde wasn't a quitter.
So he fought the fight with his a.m. transmitter.

"Your rigged cash reserve crashed while big business stashed more,
You're so pained with no gains from perpetual war.
You're pawns spawning profit in grand hands like putty,
But since I'm prepared, you declare me as nutty?"

"All our leaders are cheaters, most chosen and groomed,
Then they're told what to do. If they fold, they're entombed.
They are far from impartial to harsh Martial Laws,
And hold back our advances like tightly-packed bras."

As all history's mysteries seemed to make sense,
Clyde would humor more rumors behind his barbed fence:
"This control of the world may have gone on for years,
Puppeteering the people by preying on fears!"

"*They* claim boogeymen came, then maimed independence—,
The monsters in closets with pending attendance.
From religion to pigeon flu, *they* scare with spin—,
The most sinister prison you don't know you're in."

"If concerned with these learned New World Order events,
And you yearn overturning those tiptop percents,
We must make major plans—no man is too minor,
So let's focus our minds at the local diner."

When proud Clyde plowed inside, surrounded by truckers,
He concocted thought plots to stop the blood suckers.
Then two men traipsed inside, draped in sleeveless camo,
Bearing big burly arms—the kind with spare ammo.

"Are you Clyde? Bona fide?" The fan pried, delighted.
Clyde replied "You bet. But don't get too excited;
If we go gung-ho first, the press will dismiss this.
Pack that heat near your package—then we do business."

"We will peaceably protest and detest these crimes,
We will scatter chatter to shatter paradigms.
They have an equation. We have the solution,
To stop these atrocities: shrewd revolution."

This inspired meeting's seating required one more booth,
And the date after that—18 tables of truth.
These Greasy Spoon retreats seemed to strike a psyched chord:
As the horde's numbers soared, they could not be ignored.

When the waitress cleaned up the team's routine cuisine,
Clyde bombastically broadcasted live on the scene,
"*They're* grossly invading our days, nights, and spaces,
It's almost as if *they* are alien races!"

"*They* pump and dump poison in water to treat it,
And modify food so you slump when you eat it.
In use, both reduce IQ and fertility,
So wake for your sake; you'll see the hostility."

Drawn by transmissions of unlawful seditions,
Clyde's pack began its plans as attack tacticians,
Since incessant detest left The Spoons' heads distressed,
Clyde suggested they part and start fresh after rest.

Late, the renegade placed barricades on his gates,
As he laid booby traps to contain in dire straits.
Then he drooped on his futon with dawn's bug-out-bags,
Slumbering snugly under a number of flags.

Then from his black backyard reared a queer inbound sound,
Near his shatterproof windows on his cleared compound.
Now provoked by unknown, Clyde awoke from a tone—,
Not a bird or a plane, but a blurred and cloaked drone.

Clyde then grabbed from his stash and blasted that bastard,
And cut out its guts, peeved—yes, he had this mastered.
"I hope you hear these smears, you whores I'm maligning,
You buncha e-dwarves who adore data mining!"

"Whether naughty or nice, you spy like Old Saint Nick,
You cram cams on each street like sick, lunatic pricks.
You wiretapping psychopaths track like Big Brother,
But like thighs in tight slacks, our free rights will smother."

Soon the drone, water-boarded, it shorted and broke,
Clyde selected golf clubs and perfected his stroke.
As he gasped and collapsed near his entryway spot,
A note floated and sailed from the unused mail slot.

The note's front: a glossed coat with an all-seeing eye.
On the back: skull and crossbones. The greeting: "Comply!
Yes, as you may have guessed, we possess much to say,
So visit this address. Insincerely, from... *they*."

After Clyde's sleep attempts, his contempt for tycoons,
Made him zoom to the mansion and snoop on those goons.
"Is this a slick trick? Or could I be enlightened?
Or maybe it's me of whom *they* should be frightened?"

Clyde marched up to those arches and knocked with no plan,
When he met a warm welcome—a retina scan.
The light appeared mighty. Clyde peered through the portal.
"I enter a man. Will I exit immortal?"

When inside, shadowed figures slithered close to Clyde.
As he couldn't believe all the screens that he eyed;
They're viewing *their* doings while chewing crustaceans,
Buffets so absurd they'd sure feed third-world nations.

As the oligarchs smirked and encircled like sharks,
Like tests flunked by a dunce, *they* were all question marks.
"We've set sights on you, Clyde," an old prune confided,
"As guides, an inside job will soon be provided."

"Since we Silver Knife types do grip silver platters,
Your Greasy Spoon gripes are too trite for our matters.
You're the well-read exception, so we'll compromise,
We'll expect your affection. You'll help spread our lies."

"Take a shot. Save your spot. And you'll be immune soon,
We will scratch your back more if you act as buffoon.
We will make you so famous—a clown, world-renowned.
If you'll fake and won't shame us, your life's safe and sound."

Clyde didn't respond to the offer—just silence.
His undisclosed foes now so close to alliance:
"Return in one month once you earn the credential.
We'll run you a party. The fun's confidential."

On his next on-air test, Clyde rested on laurels,
With his designer slacks and lax repressed morals.
"I'll give you the creeps. I'll bring news that's too spooky.
It's time for the gospel according to kooky."

"Earth's flatter than pre-teen girls cleaned with steamrollers;
Those veggies you eat are destroying your molars,
And Martians so harmfully harsh with their probing,
In fact, manufacture porn of your disrobing."

"You might also read that authority's evil,
And asinine signs of decline and upheaval.
Let's all halt this assault and hope that it scatters,
Then talk lochs and lost socks. You know—stuff that matters."

From dead resurrection to astral projection,
Clyde's new-led direction provided protection.
As the butt of most jokes provoking discussions,
He shook off from the hook without repercussions:

Now, he'd double dip chips and nobody would tell;
Hotels stashed extra mints upon pillows as well.
He dismissed speeding signs and laughed at traffic stops,
And did legally litter amid throngs of cops.

Overlords, now onboard, *they* rewarded real cash,
Though submissive conditions made Clyde feel like trash.
When one week was done, he backtracked to the mansion,
To seek out the clique and then freeze his expansion.

Far inside their hangout, czars heard Clyde spouting qualms,
As he barged in and charged with drone parts in his palms.
He placed down the waste to display disgust of it,
"I'm awed by your offer. But your clan can shove it!"

"You're swank in this sanctum, but out there you're muted.
You talk like a prophet while pockets are looted.
But what more could you fancy, finance, or control?
You're schmucks running amok? What the fuck's your end goal?"

The Knives replied snidely... with their glares and disdain,
Thanking him with tranq darts to his jugular vein.
"Enough with this, Spoon!" said the chieftain prune, seething,
"We'll torment with truth then prevent you from breathing:"

"We're above and beyond cons in your government,
And we no longer ask for your low-class consent.
You are tarnished. You're harmless. Your name shamed for fame,
Like a castrated horse, your 'nay-nays' aren't the same."

"The rabbit hole's deeper. Our goal's predatory;
Big lies so disguised that no one buys the story:
We will keep some mouth-breathers here as our dumb slaves,
But most will decompose in the shallowest graves."

As Clyde fought onslaughts of supplied tranquilizers,
The globalists hissed with insistent incisors.
Rather riled, the squad smiled as prods filled *their* shill's skin,
"We're the gods with a plan and you're not penciled in!"

Flesh singeing, Clyde cringing, he yelped "Help! Attack now!
Make your move, Greasy Spoons! Let's tip this sacred cow!"
Through the hacked drone recast, Spoons awaited Clyde's dive,
As the tirade played out… on the radio live.

Spoons plunged in aware of this perilous juncture,
And picked darts from Clyde's parts like quick acupuncture.
As the grand slam program attracted more clamors,
These newly-brewed groupies could ram through the scammers.

Now outnumbered by Spoons, bigwigs blundered with fright,
Like a tree with no teeth, *their* bark's worse than *their* bite.
The Spoons bashed all those screens into smashed smithereens,
And force-fed elite mouths till each needed latrines.

Like a monsoon of hope, the Spoons blew *them* away,
No more wealth-induced stealth—just begrudged judgment day.
Now not counting *their* dough, but more so *their* losses,
Clyde led the parade of encaged former bosses.

Their team creamed the scheme and the pyramid crumbled,
With more towns to take down, the Spoons grew, but humbled.
They squared off with the parasites and left their mark,
With the right to be silent—not blind in the dark.

As the Spoons jailed those violent, Knife tyrants—now frail,
Clyde suppressed *their* requests of guest visits and quail:
"Though our blows did slow dystopian restriction,
We'll always know truth's stranger than deranged fiction."

"While our years might be cleared from the history books,
At least we took a stand reprimanding these crooks.
Believe in our treason—even if they haze me,
United despite how much *they* say we're crazy."

The movement proved it could affect a perspective.
Yet as the time passed, new recruits grew defective.
And the war raged on more with both weapon and pen,
So Clyde's diplomats had to reformat again.

As I write this outside—my eyes on that Spoon brawl,
I hope this found you well to prevent our downfall.
I trust you, future Spoon, to rightly fight the threat,
Curb and scoop out the turds—we could serve some hope yet.

Using lobbed info bombs, we hope Man understands,
Only fools crave a world that will cave in *their* hands.
But like armies of owls, *they'll* soon be in cahoots.
Want your backyard to change? Then start with some grassroots.

ACKNOWLEDGEMENTS

Thank you to my mom (Linda) for serenading me with goofy songs backed by her guitar at an impressionable age and, you know, keeping me alive for the first couple decades of my life. To my dad (Alvin) who always knew how to weave a captivating tale and, similar to Mom, exposed me to mature comedy way before I should have been. To my second set of eyes on this book and great friend John Ellerbach. To my detailed and talented illustrator Van Gia Hao. And finally, to Benjamin Fanning, Kate Fahey, and Adriana Montiel for an idea or two that I stole while talking to you about this odd project.

While I could have **totally** finished this book without any of you, it would have sucked **a lot** more. Smirk.

Pretentious Author Profile

Matthew T. McKeague hails from Lock Haven, Pennsylvania—a town known for making tiny airplanes and, uh, cutting down trees in the 1800s.

When Matt learned how to talk, he politely demanded that his Mom write down all the stories erupting from his odd head.

Later, a 5th-grade teacher told him that he was like an "even darker Steven King" after hearing his rhyming poem about shark attacks. Surprisingly, his classmates approved too. Realizing he could spread his weird thoughts without getting arrested in the process, Matt knew that writing was for him.

So Matt kept studying storytelling until he became one of those silly doctors who can't save you if you're choking on a hot dog. While doing so, he has been a reporter, video editor, video game critic, comedy writer, and professor. So what's next? President? Pope? Your Mom? Only time will tell.

Matt now spends his existence writing stories in darkened corners. He currently lives on a fictional farm with his imaginary wife and zero children.

Photos by C. Reynolds

GREETINGS FROM... THE BOOK

1. Did you like me as a book?

 YES    NO

2. You should review me. Hard. Online.

 OK!    NO!

3. Can we be friends?

  PLEASE STOP!

4. Please review me.

☐ GO AWAY!

YOUR FRIEND,
~The Book

BUT SERIOUSLY

Reviews help. Your reviews bump my book up in the search results and push my weird work in front of more potentially weird people. So, could you do me one last favor and post a review? Take one minute and visit whatever the most popular online retailer is right now with my book on it. Then post a few words about your thoughts! If that company happened to do something awful (perhaps related to clubbing seals) and you are rightfully protesting its website, then go to the second most popular site instead. Keep doing this as necessary until you hit the first website whose track record involves no seal clubbing. Oh, and if websites don't exist anymore when you're reading this, then I'll assume that robots wiped most of us out and kept a few of us around to laugh and/or stare at like a human zoo exhibit. If I'm still alive, I greatly look forward to seeing what you think in those reviews! (Yes, even from you, robot overlords.)

~Matt

OTHER BOOKS BY THIS AUTHOR

-Andy Gets Conned (2020)

Bullying in the classroom is a painful experience…especially when it's the students torturing the teacher. When history teacher Andy Gordon returns to Bumble Ridge High after summer break, he's greeted by former failed student Nathan Hader with a scheme to not only get him fired, but also ruin his nerdy life. Despite living in a town filled with killer bees, cult members, and enough corruption to be dystopian, Andy must face an even worse threat—Nathan's wrath in a classic battle of Chunky Nerd vs. Hostile Hunk. In response, Andy crafts a strategy involving geeky interests—his favorite tabletop game Rejects & Reptiles, fandom conventions, and parody musician Wacky Will Zimmerman—to try and overcome these hurdles. Will Andy prevail with his role-playing pals by his side? Or will Andy, much like the hurdles he encountered in gym class, end up faceplanting to the ground…forever?

-Dolphin Cop: Maverick from the Sea (2020)

Dolphin Cop is one badass dolphin who squeals first and asks questions later. In this comic, Dolphin Cop struggles with one cold, hard truth—he killed so many perps in town that there's no crime anymore. So Dolphin Cop takes on a small case instead, searching for the pet store's lost aardvarks. Events escalate into a whale of a tale, becoming the biggest conspiracy that Earth has ever seen. As Dolphin Cop uncovers the mystery, he stays focused the only way he knows how—spewing sea puns and blowing a lot of heads off in the process. Can Dolphin Cop turn the tides? Or will his carcass sink to the ocean floor?

OTHER BOOKS <u>NOT</u> BY THIS AUTHOR

-Hairy Otter & the Horse Fuhrer's Bones (1995)
-1984: Chicken Coup for the Proles (1949)
-The Lord of the Laundromat: Return of the Canadian Coins (1954)
-Great Expectations Lowered 'Cuz People Suck (1843)
-Shame of Scones: My Feast on Doughs (2005)
-Moby Censored: Something Big, Wet, and Deep (1851)
-Alice's Adventures in Crippling Student Debt (1862)
-Charlotte's Web of Intricately Crafted Lies Hiding an Affair (1952)
-A Wrinkle on Tim: The Aging Process Is a Real Bitch (1962)
-The Bible (Debatable)
-How to Avoid Controversy (666)
-Mein Kampf (1933)
-That One Book Series About Babysitting (1986)
-Fahrenheit 427,000: The Case of a Faulty Thermometer (1953)
-Nobody Cares About This List Anymore, Matt (1837)
-How Many More of These Are You Going to Type? (1838)
-I Think You Kinda Peaked With the Horse Fuhrer Joke (2059)
-Now You're Just Being Stubborn (1)
-Year One? Are You Kidding Me? (2)
-I'm Turning the Page Now, Matt, Goodbye (2019)

THE SECRETS OF DARKER TRUTHS

I provided my illustrator with pages upon pages of notes describing the images I needed for this book…which also included tons of hidden details. So, if you're up for a little challenge, then see if you can locate any of the following:

-The number 27 is included 9 times in this book. There's also a character wearing red and white stripes in here 9 times. Can you find them all?

-Be on the lookout for reappearing germs, gnomes, vultures, and rats.

-Every story has visual connections to the other four in some way. On repeat readings, you should start to see some neat references.

-The spoon logo is first seen in Dave's tale. And the fictitious media company Intermittent Brainwashing is featured throughout the book, starting with Dave too. Can you follow the thread?

-If you squint really hard at each picture and then post a review of the book online, then you will have posted a review online and made Matt happier. Okay, I'll stop. Promise.

Fin!

The end!

It's all over, folks!
(Why are you still here?)

Lower your expectations
because there's really nothing left.
The book's finished. I mean it!
Don't say that I didn't warn you.
Goodbye! And thanks for reading
my book, you persistent page flipper.

www.ingramcontent.com/pod-product-compliance
Lightning Source LLC
Chambersburg PA
CBHW042008150426
43195CB00002B/61